"Mark Murnan and Complete Legal Investigations, Inc. has been my law firm's exclusive investigations company for almost 20 years. Mark's creativity, follow-up, persistence, attention to detail, and care for his attorney clients have impressed me since 'day one.' As the CEO of a large personal injury law firm, I need to trust any vendor who I use, to maximize the value of my cases. I trust Mark and Complete Legal Investigations with any case, large or small, that requires detailed and complex investigative work. I highly recommend using Mark and Complete Legal Investigations if you want to provide excellent service to your clients."

-Craig Goldenfarb
Sole owner, Law Offices of Craig Goldenfarb, P.A., West Palm Beach

"Mr. Murnan is the best investigator I have worked with during my 35 years of doing personal injury work. His advice here, as always, is spot on."

- Michael S. "Mickey" Smith, Esq.
Partner, Lesser, Lesser, Landy & Smith PLLC, West Palm Beach, FL

INVESTIGATOR PROCEDURES MANUAL

MARK J. MURNAN, CLI, CFE

CERTIFIED LEGAL INVESTIGATOR
CERTIFIED FRAUD EXAMINER

WENDY STROM MURNAN, LPI, CP

LICENSED PRIVATE INVESTIGATOR
CERTIFIED PARALEGAL

PALMETTO
PUBLISHING

Charleston, SC
www.PalmettoPublishing.com

First Edition

ISBN: 978-1-7373799-0-4

ACKNOWLEDGMENTS

The authors would like to express their gratitude to the following "influencers," those who came alongside us during our careers, offering wise counsel and encouragement:

Brandon Perron, CCDI, the first PI Mark ever met who was actually making money (and a difference!) as a private investigator. Twenty months after having lunch with Brandon at a conference in 1999, Mark quit his "good government job" and launched his PI agency. Visit Brandon's site at www.defenseinvestigator.com.

Diana Garren of True Perceptions, Inc., our first consultant (and good friend), who coached us over many years and through many challenges. Through her weekly phone calls, she kept our feet to the fire and got us where we wanted to go! Visit her site at www.trueperceptions.com.

Bob Brown, an Orlando PI now deceased, who encouraged us in our early years. Rest in Christ, brother. We'll see you there.

Gary McDaniel, friend and fellow PI, who let Mark share office space with him when he got started. "Vaya con Dios," my friend!

Tim O'Rourke, friend and fellow FALI president, who took our beloved organization to new heights. (He also encouraged Mark to buy his first Milt Sparks holster!) Our love always to Tim, **Amy** and their girls.

Mary Anna Mancuso of Mav3n Digital, our social media consultant, who guided us to develop our YouTube channel, "*Investigators in Cars, Drinking Coffee*," and *The Profitable PI Series* as well. Good luck in your new city! www.mav3ndigital.com

WELCOME TO THE PROFITABLE PI© SERIES OF BOOKS AND MANUALS!

You have taken a significant step in the direction of building profitability *for* your private investigations business and taking control *of* your business. The information contained within these manuals is designed to assist you in building your infrastructure for a successful, enduring business, a business that will survive and prosper over the difficult years ahead, in good times and bad times.

I started our business in October 2001, just a few weeks after the tragic events of 9/11. My previous experience included 15 years as a staff investigator for the State Public Defender and then the Federal Public Defender, Southern District of Florida.

When Wendy left her job at a prestigious personal injury firm and joined me in September 2003, we were growing and taking on more and more cases. This was immensely satisfying, but it also caused some concerns. Our clients had come to expect consistent work product and timely responses. **Could we maintain the same level of work and response time if our business continued to grow?** It was time to get some "business-building" advice.

We developed the information in these manuals for our company, Complete Legal Investigations, Inc., beginning in 2005, when we hired our first business consultant. With the help of consultants, and many, many hours of hard work, we developed *systems, processes, and procedures* to handle our increasing caseload. From case intake to case closure, from marketing to management, and from hiring to firing, we developed these manuals and watched our business grow in size and revenue. The work was intense. Wendy and I worked all day *in* our business. On nights and weekends we worked *on* our business. These manuals were written in the midst of phone calls, interviews, dealing with staff, clients, and family. I often describe the process as trying to change a tire *while you're driving* on the Interstate!

Our goal with The Profitable PI© series is to facilitate your growth and confidence in building a sustainable, profitable business. By taking advantage of the information offered in these manuals, you will be able to write job descriptions for each of your staff members, *even if you haven't hired them yet!* Our suggestion is that you take the information offered here and apply it to your own business, rather than merely using a "cut and paste" approach. **The process of thinking through each position and procedure in light of your own vision is invaluable to your development**. Adding employees and staff members and sub-contractors is a delicate task. You must know what you expect from each member of your growing team, and *each member of your team* must know what you expect from them.

We wish you every success as you undertake this daunting, but rewarding, process. Let us know how The Profitable PI© series is helping *you* to grow *your* business!

Mark Murnan, CLI, CFE   Wendy Strom Murnan, LPI, CP
Certified Legal Investigator   *Licensed Private Investigator*
Certified Fraud Examiner   *Certified Paralegal*

Co-creators, "Investigators in Cars, Drinking Coffee" on YouTube and The Profitable PI© Series

INDEX: INVESTIGATIVE PROCEDURES

CRIMINAL DEFENSE INVESTIGATOR PROCEDURES

INVESTIGATOR CASE CHECKLIST – CRIMINAL

1. Client Interview   Date(s)
2. Case Review and Analysis
    Discovery Review
    a. Supplemental police reports
    b. State witness list
    c. Property receipts
        (1) Audio tapes/taped statements   Date req'd   Rec'd
        (2) Video tapes   Date req'd   Rec'd
        (3) Crime scene photos   Date req'd   Rec'd
        (4) Evidence reviewed (w/ attorney)   Scheduled
                                                Completed
    d. 911 tapes   Date req'd
                                                 Rec'd

Note: All requests for evidence/discovery materials must be in writing to the evidence custodian and copied to the attorney.

3. Crime Scene Examination
    a. Photos (digital)   Date_____
    b. Diagram (w/ measurements)   Date_____
    c. Aerial image (if necessary)   Date_____

4. Witnesses
    a. Prepare separate witness list, including all civilian and non-official witnesses (no police officers, fire rescue personnel, medical examiners, etc.)
    b. Obtain identifying information on each witness to include DOB, SSN, LKA, to facilitate criminal/civil background investigation
        (1) Witness list (see supplemental list attached)
        (2) Local criminal/civil history for each witness
            1. Obtain copies of P/C Aff., Information, and certified copies of criminalconvictions (judgment/sentence)
            2. Obtain financial affidavits from divorce/support files

    3.   Obtain documents from domestic assault files

    4.   Obtain copies of documents from Official Records online, including deeds and mortgages, liens, tax liens, satisfactions, etc.

(3)   Statewide criminal history-FDLE for critical witnesses

(4)   Out-of-town history (include items 1-4 in (2) above

    Assigned to   Date completed

(5)   Incident reports for critical witnesses from municipal law enforcement agencies;

(6)   Database reports for critical witnesses listing properties, former addresses, vehicles, driver licenses, associates and relatives

(7)   Booking photos - critical witnesses and co-defendants

CLIENT INTERVIEW
CRIMINAL CASE

Note: Client interview/visit is of the utmost priority. Client should be seen within 2 to 3 days of receipt of case.

1.   Identify client's location, i.e. Palm Beach County Jail, Stockade, Federal Detention Center, or out on bond.

2.   If on bond, schedule interview by phone and/or by letter.

3.   If client is incarcerated, conduct interview at facility. Confirm that attorney has sent appropriate authorization to the facility. Make sure that the attorney authorization letter is included in the investigative file.

4.   On first meeting with the client, the investigator shall provide the client with his or her business card, and explain that he is assisting the attorney with the preparation of the file for trial. NO PROMISES OR GUARANTEES SHOULD BE MADE TO THE CLIENT; all questions regarding potential plea offers should be directed to the attorney.

5.   Complete client interview form and place form on second fastener of investigative file. (Blank form will initially be located on second fastener.)

6.   Have client sign medical release and Department of Corrections release. Notarize client's signatures and place executed forms on second fastener of investigative file. (Blank forms will initially be located on second fastener.)

7.   Review the probable cause affidavit with the client. Without having the client explain what happened at the scene, ask the client to comment on each statement made in the affidavit by the arresting officer. **NOTE:** The investigator should not try to elicit a statement of guilt by the client, or any statement by the client that might preclude him or her from testifying at trial. An admission of guilt may be unavoidable or simply blurted out by the client, but no admissions should be solicited by the investigator during the initial client interview.

8.   As the client comments on the accuracy of the PC affidavit, make notes of witnesses names and identifying information for follow-up.

9.   Begin to identify possible defense issues, such as identification from a photo line-up, statements made by witnesses or the client, potential alibi witnesses, or self-defense issues.

10.   On completion of the interview, remind the client that he or she should not discuss the case with anyone, including other inmates, visitors, or family members over the phone. Explain to the client that the jail has the capacity to record telephone calls, and that other inmates frequently report statements allegedly made by clients to law enforcement or to the prosecutor to help them receive reduced sentences. Advise the client to contact the attorney's office if he or she has any questions.

11.   Do NOT leave any forms or discovery materials with the client; these items should be provided to the client by the attorney's office.

12.   Thank the client for his assistance. Assure him that his case and information will be explored fully and his witnesses will be contacted. Make sure that witness contact information is as complete as possible, including phone numbers, addresses, complete names with correct spellings, employment information, etc.

13.   After leaving the interview, whether at the jail, stockade, client's residence or attorney's office, dictate report and send to transcriptionist. Place all completed forms back into the investigative file on the second fastener.

CLIENT INTERVIEW FORM

XYZ INVESTIGATIONS, INC.

ATTORNEY WORK PRODUCT

Date and location of interview:

Identifying Information

Name and AKA's:				
DOB:		**POB:**	SSN:	
HT/WGT:	**Race:**		**M/F**	Hair/Eyes:
Tattoos or Perm. Markings:				
Perm. Address:				
HM PH:		WORK:		CELL:

Family History

Father's Name:	Age:
Address:	
Contact phone:	

Mother's Name:	Age:
Address:	
Contact phone:	

Sibling 1:
Contact phone:
Sibling 2:
Contact phone:
Sibling 3:
Contact phone:

Spouse/Significant other:
Address:
Contact phone:

Education (obtain school record authorization)

Elementary School:	
Middle School:	
High School:	
Diploma or GED/Certificate?	
Technical School:	
Certificate?	
College:	
Graduate?	Major:
Post-Graduate:	
Diagnosed LD/SLD?	Where/When?

Employment (obtain release for employment records)

Current Employer:	
Address:	
Supervisor:	
Job description:	Phone/Fax:

Unemployed at time of arrest? Y/N

Previous Employer:	
Address:	
Supervisor:	
Job Desc:	Phone/Fax:
Dates of employment:	Reason for leaving:

Workers Compensation Claims?
Employer:

Where/When:
Unemployment Claims:
Where/When:

Medical History (obtain 2-3 medical/HIPAA releases)

Physical disabilities:	
Medications:	Dosage:
Medications:	Dosage:
Hospitalizations:	
Attending physicians:	
Contact information:	
Mental health diagnoses?	
Attending psychiatrist:	
Medications:	
Substance abuse issues (Alcohol/drug):	
Treatment history (if any):	
Desire to participate in treatment program? Y/N	

Prior Criminal History

Charge #1:	
Date:	City/County/State:
Disposition (G/NG/NC/NP)	Attorney:
Sentence:	
Charge #2:	
Date:	City/County/State:
Disposition (G/NG/NC/NP)	Attorney:
Sentence:	
Charge #3:	
Date:	City/County/State:
Disposition (G/NG/NC/NP)	Attorney:
Sentence:	

If additional charges, note on separate sheet of paper.

Other information (not addressed in above form):

Version of Events (Use note paper/legal pad)
1. Review information and PC Affidavit with client
2. Without soliciting admission of guilt, determine if client has possible defense (self-defense, alibi, mistaken ID, no intent, etc.)
3. Identify potential issues to litigate (suppression, misidentification, duress)
4. Develop potential witness list with names, contact information, employment
5. Advise client not to discuss his or her case with anyone, including other inmates, family members, friends

DOCUMENTING A CRIME SCENE
CRIME SCENE CHECKLIST

1. Photograph the location, documenting the principal points of interest as outlined in the probable cause affidavit, supplemental police reports and client/witness interviews (items found in the investigative file).

2. Each photograph should be listed on a photo log depicting date/time and view of the photograph. (See sample Photo Log in this section.)

3. Prepare a rough sketch of the crime scene on a sketch form (attached as example). In certain cases, crime scene software may be available for more exact dimensions and possible court presentation. Include exterior facilities, roads and streets, driveways, street lights, traffic signals, or other items that might impact the scene or influence the ability of witnesses to make identifications.

4. The sketch should be filled out by the investigator with his name, date of the sketch, and the case name and court number.

5. Each photograph will be labeled with the date and time, the case name and number as reflected on the photo log (see sample label). The investigator's initials will also be listed on each label.

6. An aerial photograph may be provided using the Google Earth program downloaded onto the investigator's work station. Enter the subject address into the address bar on the left side menu, review the aerial photo for clarity, zoom in or out to obtain as clear a photo as possible, then print by clicking the printer icon on the lower right menu and selecting "medium print" on the print view box.

7. Write the date and investigator's name at the top of the page, the address and the case name and number below that, and the attorney-client's name below that.

8. The photographs, crime scene sketch and aerial photo will be provided to the company secretary with the accompanying photo log to be forwarded to the attorney-client. A photocopy of the photo log and crime scene sketch form will be maintained in the discovery section of the investigative file (fastener 3) by the investigator.

State v. Robert Smith
Case no. 05-13085CF A02
Prepared by Mark J. Murnan, CCDI
Attorney: Steven Schwartz, Esq.

PHOTO LOG (SAMPLE)

All photos taken April 19, 20XX by Mark Murnan, CLI

1. Cumberland Farms convenience store at 627 N Dixie Hwy, Lake Worth (SW corner of 7th Ave. No. and Dixie Hwy)

2. Close up of entrance to Cumberland Farms store

3. Entry door to Cumberland Farms depicting street address

4. Entry door to Cumberland Farms depicting hours of operation

5. Close up of hours of operation for CF store

6. Close up of hours of operation for CF store

7. NW side of CF store

8. NW side of CF store

9. Cumberland Farms store and Little Daddy's Pizza and Sub shop at 7th Ave No and Dixie Hwy from NE corner of intersection

10. Cumberland Farms store and Little Daddy's Pizza and Sub shop at 7th Ave No and Dixie Hwy from NE corner of intersection

11. Little Daddy's Pizza and Sub shop, 625-1/2 N Dixie Hwy

12. N Dixie Hwy at 7th Ave No looking south

13. N Dixie Hwy at 7th Ave No looking south

14. Majestic gas station at SE corner of 7th Ave No and Dixie Hwy

15. N Dixie Hwy at 7th Ave No looking north toward Ixora Motel (700 block)

16. Ixora Motel in 700 block of N Dixie Hwy

17. N Dixie Hwy at 7th Ave No looking south

18. Abandoned gas station at NE corner of 7th Ave No and Dixie Hwy (immed. north and across street from Majestic)

19. N Dixie Hwy at 7th Ave No looking north from east side of intersection

20. Cumberland Farms store and Little Daddy's Pizza from NE corner of intersection

21. Lake Avenue (eastbound only) at K Street, downtown Lake Worth

22. Dave's Last Resort, 600 block of Lake Ave, NE corner of Lake and K

23. Dave's Last Resort hours of operation

24. Ray's Key West Grille, 604 Lake Ave

25. Brogue's Irish Pub, 621 Lake Ave

26. 7-11 store, 100 block N Federal Hwy

27. 7-11 parking lot, N Federal Hwy looking south toward Lucerne/Lake Ave intersections

28. 7-11 parking lot, N Federal Hwy looking south toward Lucerne/Lake Ave intersections

CRIME SCENE DIAGRAM

A host of products are available for this task. Suggested resources would include forms available at http://forensic-classroom.com/forensic_downloadable_evidence_forms.php. This site provides grid forms which can then be drawn to scale, as below:

Reset Form	This form is editable - Click on the information boxes to activate			
Field Sketch—Not Drawn to Scale	Location: Aywhewre USA			
Agency: Investigative Support Specialist, Inc.	Incident: Aggravated Battery			
Drawn By: Brandon A. Perron, CCDI	Date: 01/25/2021	Time: 1:32 am	RD# 21-067-CF	

Such forms can be utilized for reference purposes for client and/or attorney meetings. They should be completed and placed into the investigative case file. These diagrams should also be supplemented with scene photos, aerial photos, and other testimonial evidence.

AERIAL PHOTOGRAPH OF SCENE

Utilizing a common map application, take an overhead view of the area surrounding the scene for the attorney's reference. Place a copy in the investigative file.

LOCATING A WITNESS

Witness Location Checklist

1. Review available reports from the investigative case file for leads to witness' current location
2. Obtain all personal identifiers, including date of birth, social security number, last known address, driver license number
3. Complete a database report (i.e. TLO, Tracers) to obtain leads to current or former addresses, vehicle registrations, property owned, relatives, employment, etc.
4. Check county records for criminal cases or traffic citations (traffic records will often include the witness' driver license number and vehicle information)
5. Check county records for civil or family/domestic violence/mental health files. Divorce files include last known addresses and employment for child support orders; domestic violence files contain physical and vehicle descriptions and employment information
6. Check with property records for any homesteaded properties, or to identify former landlords who might have a lease application with useful information.
7. DMV records are updated annually or bi-annually. See below for information.

The above checklist is only a partial list of available sources of information; the investigator and researcher should work together to develop leads in-house, and follow up those leads in the field

Materials needed

1. Proprietary database reports
2. Access to county records online

Process of investigation

In order to interview a witness, he must first be located. Often, the witness' home address and identification information (date of birth and/or social security number) will be provided in the police or incident report documenting the event being investigated. If so, locating the witness is a simple matter of confirming his residency at the address provided or perhaps confirming his employment at the location cited.

Oftentimes, the witness is no longer at the address provided, or the address was never provided to begin with. If so, the investigator will be required to locate a current address for the witness, using a combination of phone searches, databases, and public record searches.

Commercial and Proprietary Databases

Commercial databases are utilized by private investigators on a daily basis. These databases obtain information from a variety of public record sources and proprietary marketing sources. These may include everything from state motor vehicle records to mailing lists from marketing companies. Accessing these databases is often the first step in locating a witness because the databases will provide an address history for a subject, provided the witness is identified with a date of birth and/or social security number. If the date of birth or the social security number for the witness is unavailable from any records, the commercial databases should be checked for the witness' name and as close to a geographic area as possible. For instance, the name "Douglas Jenkins" is fairly common; but identifying "Douglas Jenkins" in a specific municipality within the state in question will narrow the search. If the "Douglas Jenkins" the investigator is looking for is known to be in his early thirties, most commercial databases will allow a search to be run by name within a specific age range. Using this process of elimination on some preliminary searches can help to identify the specific Douglas Jenkins the investigator is looking for.

Sometimes a witness' name is misspelled or his date of birth is inaccurately reflected on the report. The databases can assist in obtaining the correct information.

Department of Motor Vehicles

In Florida, the Department of Highway Safety and Motor Vehicles maintains vehicle registration information and driver license information. This information is considered "public record," yet can only be accessed via a courthouse or tax collector office, or through a contracted database service, such as Auto Data Direct (ADD123.com). This "real time" resource can be accessed by licensed investigators to run a vehicle search by owner, a license tag noted in a crash report or on a database report, or to determine the status of a driver's license or actual driving history.

Search Engines and Browsers

The best example of a non-proprietary database search would include a simple Google search (or another browser). A name search via this browser may disclose social media pages, news articles, or general information to assist with the search. It is free and can be a time-saving shortcut, similar to an old telephone listing search.

Social Media Searches

So many people are on social media that this is often a primary means of identifying or locating witnesses, civil defendants, or other parties. Searches via Facebook, Instagram, Twitter, or the dozens of other platforms that are always emerging can be daunting. A social media search engine such as Skopenow.com can help identify a subject, or narrow down several subjects for a more manageable search.

Remember that databases and online searches are no substitute for field investigation and should be considered only as a research tool. For instance, many databases update their source information several times per year, but if the witness has moved in the past two to three months, that information may not show up in the time that you are trying to locate the individual. Keep in mind that an address history is not necessarily accurate and should be confirmed before entering such an address in the final report.

Often, the database information will reflect several subjects residing at the same residence. **The investigator should confirm the residency of any individuals at the given address with a phone call or a field investigation.**

Verify any information provided in a database report with a telephone call or a visit to the address, or contacting the source of information provided in the report, especially when it reflects criminal or civil court actions. For instance, it would be a mistake to assume that the "Douglas Jenkins" you located and obtained a database report on actually filed for bankruptcy without confirming the bankruptcy record through the bankruptcy court in the jurisdiction reflected in the database report. **Again, all information obtained through a database report should be confirmed independently before entering it into the final report.**

Public Records and Courthouse Searches

If no current or recent address can be developed through either phone listings or database searches, the next step will require a more in depth search at the courthouse in the jurisdiction the witness was last believed to reside in. The investigator should be familiar enough with her own courthouse that she can find her way around the various sources of public records information:

- Felony and misdemeanor clerks' offices;
- Upper and lower civil court clerks' offices;
- Mental health, probate, family and domestic violence clerks' offices.
- Tax collector's office.
- Property Appraiser's office.

Most clerk's offices have online access that can be accomplished without actually traveling to the courthouse. Some records, however, cannot be viewed without visiting the clerk's office (e.g. family court cases such as divorce and custody files, domestic violence cases).

Records maintained at the county courthouse are usually available for a free review, and examining these court files will provide not only location, but additional background information on your witness that could be beneficial to your attorney/client. (See the procedure on background investigations and courthouse searches for additional information.)

Police Incident Reports

Some witnesses are very transient or may be in frequent contact with law enforcement. Law enforcement agencies should be contacted through their records department, and name searches can be conducted to determine if the witness has been named in any reports, either as a complainant or suspect. While public records law varies from state to state, many states and municipalities will release these reports for a nominal fee.

By systematically checking for recent traffic citations, misdemeanor arrests, divorce and child support files, and even small and large civil claims, almost anyone can eventually be located.

Field Investigation

For those witnesses who cannot be located immediately, or to confirm information developed by the processes above, a field investigation may be required. Once the address list is compiled, along with the most current vehicle registrations and names of the potential landlords, the field investigator will begin a search of the subject at the last known or developed addresses. These locations would include former addresses where the subject may have lived; places of employment found either in court records or database sources;

places frequented by the subject as determined by those same sources; the purpose being to eliminate those locations as current or non-current. In most instances, the interviews conducted at these locations will involve the presentation of the investigator's business card, a brief explanation that the investigator is attempting to locate a witness to an incident, and request for assistance by providing either the subject's current location or last known location or place of employment. Included in the request should be a request about other parties living with the subject. Does he or she have a girlfriend or boyfriend that they are living with? Did the police ever respond to that address? Is the subject married or does he have children residing with him? In other words, the field interview should be conducted in order to "fill in the blanks" with as much information about the subject as possible. Often, the subject cannot be located directly, but a former landlord or neighbor or current resident may be able to provide information about other individuals residing at the location.

Case Study

On one occasion, the investigator had a police report and database reports which indicated a witness lived in an apartment approximately 50 miles from the office. The phone numbers for the witness had been disconnected, and there was no employer known. The investigator had another case in the same vicinity which could be worked at the same time (an important time-saving consideration), so one afternoon he stopped by the witness' last known address and found it to be an apartment building with about 40 units. He went to the address listed for the witness, and there was no answer when he went to the door. Next door, however, he found an elderly woman who told him that the witness had moved out. The investigator made sure that she had his business card and saw his state-issued identification so that she felt comfortable talking to him. After checking his identification and engaging in a brief conversation, she invited him into her home and told him that his witness had moved out of state, and that she had a phone number for him. Not only did she provide this phone number, but she also gave the investigator the witness' wife's name and explained that the witness happened to leave the state for a better job in construction in the new location. After visiting with her for a few minutes, she disclosed that she was 97 years old and was very proud of her continued mental acuity. They had a friendly visit for a few minutes, the investigator thanked her for her time, and returned to his office, where he called the witness. He found the witness at home and took a complete statement from him.

<u>Friends and Family</u>

Another technique in locating witnesses during the field investigation is by identifying relatives and associates through the database report and social media pages. Oftentimes, public records, police reports, and database reports will name parties associated with the witness, including spouses (or ex-spouses), neighbors, parents, or other relatives. Part of the field investigation will include contact with these other parties, either in person or by telephone.

Case Study

While conducting a background investigation of a man who had recently taken up with the client's wife, incident reports had been obtained by the police agency for the municipality the man lived in. The police reports named two women the subject had been involved with. One of the women was located using a database report and interviewed by telephone. The other woman had moved from a last known address, and her current location was unknown. The first woman knew the second woman and that she had located to another town in the center of the state. Careful examination of one of the incident reports provided by the municipal law enforcement agency revealed that the second woman's father had called the police to conduct a welfare check of his daughter at her last known address. With the woman's father name now known, a review of the database report reflected his name, address, and home telephone number in a northern state. A telephone call was placed to this number, and a woman who identified herself as the woman's mother answered the phone. The investigator explained the reason for the call, the mother took the investigator's name and phone number, and agreed to forward the information to her daughter, the woman the investigator was trying to locate. Within 24 hours, the woman contacted the investigator, and information about the woman and her relationship was obtained in a telephone interview.

Surveillance

Another type of field investigation might include surveillance of a location that the witness frequents in order to develop a residential address for service of process or subsequent interview. Surveillance is physically demanding and time intensive, but there may be no other means of locating the witness. If a neighborhood canvas has indicated that the subject is at the residence infrequently, then surveillance may be the only way to determine when the subject is at the address.

Case Study

A hostile witness in a pending lawsuit had been completely uncooperative with opposing counsel and was making himself "hard to find." The investigator was asked to locate an address where the subject could be served with a summons, as he was not only a witness, but a named party. Database reports indicated the subject had a local address, as well as an address located in a small fishing village approximately 80 miles away. Periodic surveillance at the local address did not succeed in locating the client or the vehicle he was known to be driving. Early one morning, an investigator and an associate, who was familiar with the witness, drove to the fishing village 80 miles away. The database report provided a street address, which was checked at approximately 7:30 a.m., without locating the subject, but a trailer registered to the subject was at the address. Surveillance was set up on the location, and approximately 45 minutes later, the witness drove up in the truck that was registered in his name. The investigator's associate recognized the witness, and surveillance continued on the witness, who stayed at the fishing village address for a short time before beginning the long drive back to the investigator's city. Constant visual contact was maintained with the witness' vehicle, and as he drove into the city limits, the investigator contacted the attorney, who arranged for a process server to rendezvous with the investigator at the witness' ultimate destination. Sure enough, after a couple of stops, the witness drove to the local address, parked his truck and went inside the residence, leaving the front door open. A few minutes later, the process server arrived and met with the investigator, who accompanied the process server to the front door, where the witness was served with a summons initiating the lawsuit.

Conclusion

These case studies provide several examples of the investigation necessary to locate witnesses, including phone listings, database reports, and public records searches, as well as subsequent field investigation and surveillance. Sometimes all elements of a search are required to locate "hard to find" witnesses. The ultimate success of the investigation will depend on the investigator's knowledge of basic search procedure, persistence, endurance, and resourcefulness.

WITNESS INTERVIEWS (CRIMINAL)

Witness statements in criminal cases differ from civil cases in that the interview is not necessarily recorded. In fact, only if a witness offers clearly exculpatory testimony (offering evidence of lack of guilt) and the investigator suspects that the witness may change his or her testimony subsequent to the interview, should the investigator consider recording the witness' statement.

Generally, witness interviews in criminal cases are conducted in person, often at the witness' residence during a field investigation. Witness names (in state court) and addresses are provided by the State Attorney handling the prosecution on a list, which includes civilian, law enforcement and other witnesses, including fire-rescue or medical examiner personnel. Witness names and contact information is not generally provided in federal court.

State court witnesses
Review the witness list provided in discovery and the police reports for statements made by the witness. According to the Component Method™, witness interviews are conducted after completion of the crime scene examination (to familiarize the investigator with the location and features of the event) and the witness background investigation (to determine the criminal history, if any, of the witness). With this familiarity and background, the investigator should be prepared to question each civilian witness about his or her observations of the event, and to determine if there are any discrepancies between earlier statements, current comments, and the physical location of the crime scene (observing an action from a window that doesn't exist, for instance).

Avoiding misidentification
It is a felony in some jurisdictions to impersonate a law enforcement officer. It is also misrepresentation to allow a witness to conclude that a private investigator is, in fact, a law enforcement officer, by neglecting to inform the witness of the investigator's real status. When meeting a witness for the first time, your identification as a defense investigator is critical. Some witnesses will listen to you as you identify yourself as a private investigator, will look at your business card, and swear under oath several months later that the investigator they spoke to claimed he was a law enforcement officer. After several years of walking this dicey line and seeing a co-worker have to defend himself against a charge of witness tampering, I developed a simple strategy that I learned at a conference: using my business card twice.

During witness interviews of government or state witnesses, I made it a habit to give my card to the witness on introduction. I stated clearly that I was working for the attorney who represented the defendant. After the interview, I would often conclude the interview by reminding the witness who I worked for, asking if he or she still had my business card, and then pulling out a second business card! I then asked the witness if he or she would simply initial the back of the card for me, explaining that I didn't want there to be any confusion later on about who I worked for. Once I had secured the witness's initials on the back of the second card, I taped the initialed card in my case file for future reference, if the issue of misrepresentation ever came up. Surprisingly, after initiating this practice, it never did.

Civilian and official witnesses

Interviews are generally limited to civilian witnesses, since official (law enforcement, fire-rescue) witnesses will usually decline to provide an interview prior to deposition (a formal examination of the witness provided under oath at the request of the defense attorney with the prosecutor present). Although nothing precludes the investigator from contacting a law enforcement officer prior to deposition for an interview, and sometimes it is necessary to do so to obtain discovery materials, most often the attorney will ask the investigator to concentrate on the more available (and informative) civilian witnesses.

Civilian witnesses often were present at the event in question, or have specific knowledge related to the event, either from statements made by the defendant or the victim before or after the event. In addition to the information the witness might offer, the attorney is also interested in the investigator's observations about the witness himself: Is he credible? A drug addict? An alcoholic? Unemployed? How does she appear? Clean and neat, or sloppy in appearance and recollection? Will she favorably impress a jury, or turn them off because of poor hygiene? It is this valuable information that provides the defense attorney with a slight edge in his or her calculations in trial preparation.

The interview

After identification and initial observation, begin by asking the witness to provide a narrative of his or her knowledge of the event. Be aware of any discrepancies in the witness' version and what the reporting officer has put into the police report. Ask the witness to "flesh out" his story by explaining his location at the scene, his interaction with other witnesses or the defendant or victim. Question about the witness about his activities at the time of the event, as well as immediately before. How did the witness happen to be at the event? How did he get there and who did he arrive with? Question him about his level of intoxication: Had he been drinking beforehand? If the investigator knows the witness has a drug history, ask if the witness had been using drugs. Sometimes witnesses will make admissions if difficult questions are asked with some empathy and friendliness.

The demeanor of the investigator is crucial to a successful interview. Since the private investigator has no true "authority," it makes little sense to use intimidation or harshness while trying to obtain information from witnesses who have no real obligation to cooperate. On the other hand, sometimes a brusque or cooly professional attitude is appropriate when dealing with certain types of personalities. The investigator will have to develop his or her "people-reading" skills and learn to select the proper "tool" from the relational toolbox to obtain interviews from a variety of witness personalities.

Note-taking

Handwritten notes should be maintained in the investigative file, preferably in one section. These notes will provide the material for dictating the report, and may occasionally be the subject of a hearing, so careful note-taking is an important process. The notes should include the date of the interview, location where the interview occurred, and the witness's name and contact information. Notes regarding the subject matter should be decipherable to the investigator (not necessarily anyone else!).

DEVELOPING A TIME LINE

Time Line Checklist

1. Using facts from the probable cause affidavit and discovery materials, make a list of all dates and times on a legal pad.

2. Arrange all facts chronologically by date and time on a word processing document.

3. Mark the time line with the name of the case and the court case number; the name of the investigator compiling the time line; and the sequential number of the time line (1, 2, 3, etc) as the time line will be amended with new information.

4. Maintain a photocopy of the time line in the discovery section of the file (fastener 3).

5. The investigator shall provide the original time line to the secretary with a report noting the case name and court case number, the date the time line was compiled, and the date it was sent to the attorney-client.

6. As new facts are uncovered, amend the time line to reflect the new information.

7. Provide the attorney-client with updated time lines, marked with the same information as indicated in paragraph 3 and the sequential number of the amended time line (Jones TL #2, amended 6/1/06). This should be sent via the secretary with a short report noting the amended time line was forwarded to the attorney-client.

REPORT PREPARATION (CIVIL AND CRIMINAL)

It is the policy of XYZ Investigations, Inc., that staff investigators dictate reports of all activities conducted during the course of assigned investigations. It is impractical and non-productive for a professional investigator to sit and type reports when resources are available to type and review a dictated report.

1.   The investigator takes notes from the completed interview or task. Using the company provided digital recorder, the investigator will dictate, in a narrative style, the content of the information obtained. Review the **Format** for each particular report type, i.e. assets check, client/witness interview, field canvass.

     a.   The attorney's name shall be provided, along with the case reference, i.e.: "*This report is for Mitchell Beers, Esq. The case reference is State v. Mahoney, case number 2018CF1040A. This is an interview of Warren Stafford.*" (It is not necessary to provide the attorney's address, since the transcriber usually has this information.)

     b.   The narrative shall follow the report **format**, samples of which are included in this manual.

     c.   The signature line shall be provided at the end of the report: "*Submitted by Michael Jones, Licensed Private Investigator.*"

2.   Reports shall be compiled in a single digital file for transfer to the transcriptionist.

3.   Reports shall be forwarded, via e-mail, to the transcriptionist at the end of each business day.

4.   Once the reports have been typed, the transcriptionist shall e-mail the draft reports to the investigator for review.

5.   The investigator shall review and make any changes to the draft report.

6.   Once the review has been completed, the report shall be e-mailed to the office manager and placed into the "drafts" computer folder for review by the office manager.

7.   Once the office manager has reviewed the reports for grammar and punctuation, the case manager will next review the reports for content and form and place the completed reports into the "Proofs" computer folder for printing and mailing.

8.   The administrative assistant will print the reports, make copies of the reports for the investigative file, fax and/or mail the reports to the recipient, being sure to include all enclosures.

9.   The administrative assistant will file a copy of the report in the investigative file.

COURT TESTIMONY

Overview: An investigator may have to provide sworn testimony in court or at deposition. Her appearance, demeanor, knowledge and reliability will be observed carefully by the client, opposing counsel, and the court. Preparation and confidence are critical to a successful presentation of the investigator's testimony.

Preparation: The investigator will be advised by the attorney-client well in advance of the event that she may be a witness to a particular aspect of the case. It may be to provide testimony related to an interview, or to present photographs of a crime scene into evidence, or to relate to the court about specific aspects of the investigation.

Preparation for testimony includes the following:
1.   Review the case file to familiarize yourself with all the issues being litigated.

2.   Review all written reports and field notes related to the investigation.

3.   Review any photographs, charts, diagrams, videos or statements taken during the investigation, or prepared for the hearing.

4.   Meet with the attorney-client to discuss the scope and focus of your testimony. Make sure you are clear on what will be testified to, and what aspects of the investigation are not to be discussed. This will be up to the attorney, as he will conduct the direct examination.

On the day of your appearance:
1.   Wear business attire suitable to the event. If your deposition is to be taken, a shirt and tie for men, or slacks/skirt and dress shirt/blouse for women should be worn. A sport coat may be advisable for men, but a formal suit is not necessary. For court hearings or trial, men should wear a (dark) suit and tie, women should wear a suit (preferably dark) and tailored blouse.

2.   Personal grooming is particularly important while testifying. Conservative hair styles and neatness are in order. Refrain from wearing excessive jewelry or glamorized accessories. Allow nothing to interfere or draw away from your presentation of your testimony.

3.   Arrive at least thirty minutes prior to your scheduled deposition in order to meet with the attorney. Many clients will schedule a meeting in advance of the deposition or hearing in order to review your testimony, but on the day of the hearing or deposition, the client will also want to have a few minutes in advance to refresh your recollections and provide you with any new information that might be addressed.

Testifying:

1. Testimony is provided to the hearer of fact, either opposing counsel or the court, while the investigator is sworn under oath. It is imperative that everything stated in your testimony is completely truthful, in response to the question being asked.

2. Testimony is comprised of the following processes: Direct examination: The attorney-client who has called you to testify will ask questions related to your investigation that pertains to the aspect of the case you are being presented for. Cross-examination: The opposing counsel will question you about information presented during direct examination. In deposition, the opposing counsel has the ability to ask more broad questions, not necessarily limited to the matter you are being called for. In trial, opposing counsel is limited to questions related to your direct examination. Re-direct: The attorney-client can clarify your answers from cross-examination, or have you repeat testimony from your direct examination.

3. Listen carefully to the questions being asked, leaving space before answering in order to respond appropriately.

4. Do not elaborate on answers, unless asked to do so by the attorney-client. In responding to opposing counsel, do not elaborate: have the attorney ask more specific questions.

5. If in doubt about a question, ask for clarification from the questioning attorney. Do not guess, offer opinion, or provide any information unless you are certain about the question. If you are confused by the question (not uncommon with some attorneys), ask the attorney to please repeat the question. Restate the question so you are certain.

6. In trial, do not address your answers to the attorneys, but to the jury or the judge. The judge or jury is the fact-finder.

7. Bring your file with you, but do not take it to the stand unless instructed to do so by the client. You may be offered documents or photographs to review or authenticate for presentation to the jury or judge. Review each document thoroughly, and place them in front of you for further review if questioned. The attorney presenting the exhibits may ask questions about the exhibits, then present them to the judge or jury upon permission from the court.

8. At all times, avoid argument, criticism, or aggressive behavior on the witness stand. You are there as an impartial witness, with no side to take in the litigation. Opposing counsel may try to bait you or harass or embarrass you with leading questions or criticism of your investigation. By staying cool under fire, you will elicit respect for your testimony by the judge and jury. If unable to answer a question, simply state, "I don't know." If opposing counsel asks if you did something, and you did not, simply state that you did not. Don't offer excuses or make something up to cover yourself. Don't try to explain something to make yourself look better. Allow the attorney-client to clear up any issues he feels is important during re-direct examination.

9. When making presentations to the jury or judge, using photographs or charts and diagrams, you may be asked to step away from the witness stand. Wait for direction from the attorney and the court before making any statements. Speak in a clear voice to the judge or jury. Use whatever tools are available, such as a pointer or laser device, to assist you in your presentation. Make eye contact with the judge or jury members. On completion, wait for further instructions or questions from the court. As instructed, return to the witness chair on completion of the presentation.

10. After direct, cross-examination, presentations and re-direct, the attorneys will be done with their questioning of you. The judge will ask the attorneys if you can be released, and on their acknowledgment, the judge will release you from the witness stand.

Testifying in court can be challenging, but by maintaining your demeanor and objectivity, your presentation can greatly benefit the attorney-client in the litigation of his case.

COURTHOUSE RESEARCH

The courthouse contains records that are available to the public to review and copy. Our cases often require a physical review of these court documents, and it is often necessary to obtain copies of these documents.

Certified copies are copies of documents from the court files which are certified by the Clerk's staff as being genuine copies from the original court file. In order for the document to be introduced in court, the clerk's certification is required. The clerk's certification consists of a blue ink stamp, along with the Clerk's signature, affixed to the document.

There are several offices within the courthouse where we routinely obtain documents. These include **Circuit/Criminal (Felony), County/Criminal (Misdemeanor-Traffic), Circuit/Civil (Lawsuits), Circuit/Domestic (Family), County/Civil (Small Claims), Probate/Mental Health, Indexing and Photocopy**. (Names of offices may vary from state to state.) We will describe what each office contains.

Circuit/Criminal (Felony)
This office contains felony criminal court files maintained by divisions. *Divisions* each have a circuit judge assigned, with a judicial assistant and clerks assigned to maintain the court files. Felony cases include serious violations of the law, either violent crimes (sexual battery, murder, armed robbery, carjacking), property/theft crimes (burglary, grand theft) or drug crimes (possession/trafficking in cocaine/heroin/marijuana) .

Felony court files contain the following documents:

1.   Information: the original charging document containing the specific allegation(s) and violation(s) of state statute.

2.   Probable cause affidavit: also called arrest affidavit or "A" form in different jurisdictions, this document outlines the specific acts allegedly committed by the defendant that constitute "probable cause" for his or her arrest. It will contain the name of the investigating officer, the defendant, the alleged victim, any co-defendants or witnesses, the date, location and time of the alleged offense and will provide a brief summary of the police investigation.

3.   Discovery list: provided by the State Attorney (prosecutor), this will include the state's witness list, a list of items obtained by law enforcement during their investigation which will be introduced as evidence (taped statements, videos, photo line-ups, 911 tapes, weapons, etc.).

4.   Motions and orders: these will be filed by the defense attorney and prosecutor and relate to issues being litigated during the pre- and post-trial stage of the case.

5.   Docket sheets: these are compiled by the courtroom clerk and document the actions taken by the court at each hearing.

6.   Disposition: these include the following documents which record the settlement of the criminal case:

    a.   Plea sheets: in case of a settlement offer made by the state, these documents will record the defendant's criminal history, the points ascribed to the defendant for his criminal history, the charge to which the defendant will plead guilty, and the attorneys representing the state and the defendant.

    b.   Judgment: the order by the court noting the defendant's plea or conviction, the finding that the defendant plead guilty to the charge specified in the judgment, and whether the client was adjudicated guilty or adjudication was withheld. A fingerprint card recording the defendant's fingerprints will be included where the defendant is adjudicated guilty.

    c.   Sentence: a separate document noting the length of incarceration in the Department of Corrections or the county jail, and any subsequent requirements such as community control or probation, fines, and any other restrictions placed on the defendant. This document will also include a reference to "time served" by the defendant prior to sentencing on the instant charge, which is usually credited against the sentence to incarceration.

    d.   Orders of Probation: Should the defendant be sentenced to a time of probation rather than incarceration, the judge will issue an order of probation in lieu of a sentencing order. This order will specify the length of probation, the specific charge for which the probationer has been sentenced, and the terms of the probation, including requirements for payment of court costs and restitution, drug or alcohol treatment, curfews or other restrictions, and possible no contact orders for the victim or witnesses.

    e.   Violation of Probation: this affidavit is submitted by the probation officer supervising the probationer and alleges specific actions committed by the probationer in violation of the orders of probation. These actions will include the following types of violations:

        i.   *Substantive violations*: violations which involve specific acts such as new criminal charges;

        ii.   *Technical violations*: violations including failure to pay court costs or probation costs, failure to submit required monthly reports, moving or changing employment without notifying the probation officer.

County/Criminal (Misdemeanor-Traffic)

This office maintains misdemeanor criminal and traffic cases by division. These cases are assigned to county court judges, with judicial assistants and clerks assigned to each division. The volume of cases in county criminal court is significantly higher than in felony cases and the cases are less serious in nature than in circuit criminal (felony) court. Misdemeanor cases include petit theft, possession of marijuana (under 20 grams), possession of narcotic paraphernalia, battery (domestic or simple); traffic cases include speeding or other violations, driving under suspended license, improper or broken equipment, failure to maintain required insurance.

Driving Under the Influence (DUI), also called *Driving While Intoxicated (DWI)* may be found in the misdemeanor/traffic clerk's office. When the violation results in an injury or death, the case may be filed in felony court by the prosecutor.

Misdemeanor court files contain the following documents:

1.   Information: See item #1 under felony court. (Note: Informations may not be filed in all misdemeanor cases; if one is not contained in the court file, it may have been filed directly from the PC affidavit.)

2.   Probable cause affidavit: See item #2 under felony court.

3.   Discovery lists: See item #3 under felony court.

4.   Motions and orders: See item #4 under felony court.

5.   Docket sheets: See item #5 under felony court.

6.   Disposition: not as comprehensive as item #6 under felony court, since defendants cannot be sentenced to prison. Convictions will result in more simplified orders including probation, or incarceration in the county jail for less than twelve months.

Traffic court files contain the following documents:

1.   Traffic citations issued by law enforcement officers.

2.   Hearing officer notes (if any).

3.   Docket sheet reflecting the disposition by the hearing officer or judge.

4.   Defendant's driving record.

Circuit/Civil (Lawsuits)
This office contains civil lawsuits which allege damages in excess of a certain amount, usually $10,000. These suits include auto collisions resulting in injuries, breach of contract, defamation, and other civil

litigation. They are assigned by division to a circuit court judge, with a judicial assistant and clerks responsible for maintaining the court file.

Circuit civil cases include the following documents:

1.   Complaint: this multi-page document contains the allegations made by the plaintiff against certain actions taken by the defendant which resulted in injuries or other losses to the plaintiff.

2.   Answer: filed by the defendant in response to the complaint, and explaining why the defendant is not responsible for the damages alleged by the plaintiff.

3.   Cross-complaint: filed by the defendant in some cases and containing allegations made by the defendant against certain actions taken by the plaintiff which resulted in injuries or other losses to the defendant.

4.   Interrogatories and Requests to Produce: filed by the complaining party against the defendant, demanding specific records and answers to specific questions related to the alleged loss.

5.   Affidavits: filed by either party in response to an order by the judge.

6.   Notice of dismissal: filed by either party in response to a settlement agreement or other disposition.

Circuit/Domestic (Family/Domestic Violence)
This office oversees cases assigned by division to family court judges who hear cases involving divorce, child custody, domestic violence, and support issues.

Circuit domestic cases include the following documents:

1.   Petition: this is the initial document filed by the party initiating the domestic action, either for divorce or an injunction against domestic violence.

2.   Financial affidavit: filed by both parties outlining their financial status, including employment income, savings and investment accounts, vehicles owned, secured and unsecured debt (mortgages, credit cards), real estate holdings, business assets, monthly expenses and obligations, child care costs and other expenses.

3.   Property settlement agreement: outlines the obligations of both parties pursuant to the final judgment of divorce.

4.   Final judgment: order of the court dissolving the marriage of the parties, and incorporating the property settlement agreement.

5.   Income deduction order: filed by the court ordering payment of child support and/or alimony to the eligible spouse and primary custodial parent. This order will include the name and address of the payee's employer.

County/Civil (Small Claims)

This office contains civil lawsuits which allege damages in amounts less than those filed in circuit civil court. These suits include some auto collisions, landlord/tenant disputes and evictions, breach of contract, defamation, and other civil litigation. They are assigned by division to a county court judge, with a judicial assistant and clerks responsible for maintaining the court file.

County court cases include the following documents:

1.   Complaint: like the document filed in circuit civil lawsuits, this document outlines the damages incurred by the plaintiff which form the basis for the suit. Since the amounts involved are generally significantly less than circuit civil, and often the parties do not have attorneys representing them, complaints in county court may be written on a generic form like a notice of eviction, or even handwritten.

2.   Answer: submitted by the defendant in response to the complaint.

3.   Order: filed by the court recording the judgment of the court and finding for or against the plaintiff.

Probate/Mental Health

This office is responsible for administering cases involving probate, mental health, and civil confinements for drug and/or alcohol abuse.

Probate and mental health cases include the following documents:

1.   Petition: filed by the representative for the decedent or a family member requesting the court to take action to probate the decedent's estate or admit an individual into emergency treatment for alcohol (Baker Act) or drug (Marchman Act) abuse.

2.   Recommendation: filed by the hearing officer who reviews the facts of the case and making recommendations regarding the estate or urging confinement of the subject to emergency treatment.

Indexing/Photocopy

This office maintains documents for copying and review by the public. Court files eventually are reduced to microfilm and microfiche and maintained in retrievable format which can be ordered and made into paper copy. Land records and purchases are recorded and reviewed by title company employees.

Official records are available online, but when printed from the Web site, are imprinted with the notice that the document is not an official copy. Documents obtained from this office do not have the imprint and are considered "official" for production and use in court or other venues.

Documents available at this office include deeds, mortgages, liens, judgments (civil and criminal), affidavits, satisfactions, tax liens, and others. Plat books are also available, containing original property boundaries and surveys.

LAW ENFORCEMENT PERSONNEL/IA REVIEWS

During background investigations on arresting officers, a review of the officer's personnel and internal affairs files will be beneficial. A request to review the file should be made in writing and faxed/mailed to the Human Resources and Internal Affairs offices of the employing agency (see Discovery Requests–Initial file folders for these letters). On acknowledgment by the agency/department, schedule an appointment to review the files in person.

At the agency, schedule sufficient time for a thorough examination of the file(s). Mark each page to be photocopied with a paper clip or post-it note, whichever the agency utilizes for this purpose. Take sufficient cash from petty cash for the cost of the copies, and ask the department in advance the cost per page.

The following documents from the respective department files should be reviewed:

Human Resources:

1. Application for employment: Determine where these individuals have worked before and their reasons for leaving their former employment. You can obtain copies of the application for the file.

2. Training records: What training have these officers received? Make a note of the various courses taken.

3. Disciplinary actions: Have any of these officers received disciplinary reports? Are there any reports of excessive violence? Pay attention to any mention of falsifying a report, whether it had to do with an arrest or a simple car crash. What were they disciplined for? Any suspensions, reduction in rank, removal from current assignments?

4. Letters of commendation: These consist of "ataboys" from members of the community who have written the agency to compliment the service of the officer. They have some value in providing insight into the officer at his or her best.

5. Performance evaluations: These annual or semi-annual reports are invaluable in documenting the performance of the officer over a period of time. Most officers will, at one time or another, run across a supervisor who is less than complimentary and may document circumstances that another supervisor was unwilling to address. Issues such as dishonesty, short-cutting, questionable tactics, exaggeration, laziness, or insubordination can be found in these records. Make careful note of the comments by the supervisor, and obtain copies of any report which may be relevant to your inquiry. Pay particular attention to evaluations which precede or immediately follow a transfer to a new unit or assignment to determine the circumstances that lead to the change.

6. Payroll records and income deduction orders: Payroll records reflect the progressive salary increases an officer receives during his or her tenure within the department. Child support orders may be found requiring the agency to deduct an amount for support from every paycheck. Note the jurisdiction and case number, as this will lead to additional information from a divorce or paternity court file.

Internal Affairs:

Internal Affairs investigates allegations of violations of agency policy and/or procedures, criminal activities, officer shootings, officer misconduct, and malfeasance by agency employees. Allegations may originate with citizens, supervisors, or other officers. Investigations are initiated with a complaint form, citing the allegations, the name of the complainant, and the dates, times and locations the alleged activity occurred, if known. The file will contain narrative reports, transcripts of recorded statements, supplemental reports and conclusions by the investigating officer, and a disposition by the head of Internal Affairs. The dispositions are SUSTAINED, NOT SUSTAINED, UNSUBSTANTIATED, UNFOUNDED. *Sustained* reports indicate a finding against the officer and disciplinary action taken. *Not sustained* means there was no finding, although there were indicators; *Unsubstantiated* means there was no way to corroborate the allegations; *Unfounded* means there was no basis found for the allegations. A final conclusion may consist of any action from a letter of reprimand to a recommendation that the officer/employee be fired and/or charged criminally. The final disposition will be signed by a ranking or senior staff member, up to the head of the agency (Chief/Sheriff). Obtain copies of **dispositions** where the complaints were SUSTAINED, and make note of any reports that may be relevant to your inquiry, regardless of disposition. It may also be possible to obtain, in advance, a list of cases the officer has in IA, with a summary of the allegation and the disposition. This document can be very helpful in ascertaining the need for a personal review.

1. Determine the status of any internal affairs investigations.
2. Obtain copies of any reports relevant to your inquiry, including the disposition and the letter/memo dictating the final outcome.
3. Obtain copies of any dispositions where the allegations were SUSTAINED, regardless of the type of case. Include a copy of the original complaint, the findings of the investigating officer, and the letter/memo from the ranking officer citing the findings and specifying the penalties.

Out-of-town Agencies: In cases in which the law enforcement agency is out of town, it may be more cost effective to request copies of the entire personnel file, especially if the agency is 50 or more miles away. The cost to copy and ship the records is far less than the investigative time and travel required for the review. This should be discussed, however, with the Case Manager, on a case by case basis.

Conclusion: Take good notes, obtain copies of any interesting documents (application, letters of discipline, IA dispositions, etc.) You may have to pay for the copies, so have some petty cash with you.

CIVIL LIABILITY INVESTIGATOR PROCEDURES

FIELD INVESTIGATOR CASE CHECKLIST – CIVIL LIABILITY

1.   Receive assignment from case manager from listed tasks:
   (a)   Locate witnesses (see page 22-25)
   (b)   Recorded witness statements
   (c)   Crash scene and crash vehicle investigations
   (d)   Report preparation

2.   Prepare reports and photo logs for attorney and forward to transcriptionist.

CIVIL CASE RECORDED WITNESS STATEMENTS

Witness statements and civil cases from our plaintiff attorney clients are generally recorded. A recorded witness statement utilizing the Olympus recorder provided to the investigators will be obtained. It will be necessary for the investigator to contact the witness by telephone, if not done in person. The format will be as follows:

1) Introduction: The investigator will contact the witness at the developed phone number and identify himself or herself as a private investigator working on behalf of the plaintiff for the plaintiff's attorney. The introduction should be used as a means to explain the purpose for the call, to identify the investigator as calling on behalf of the plaintiff, and to establish the relationship between the plaintiff and the witness, if there is one. Oftentimes, the witness will have no previous relationship with plaintiff, such as a witness to a vehicle collision. This should be established during the course of the introduction. Permission for recording a taped statement should be obtained, using verbiage such as, "Mrs. Jones, I would like to take a recorded statement from you to memorialize our conversation. It will just take a few minutes of your time. Do I have your permission to do so?" The recording device should already be set up to the phone via a digital patch or ear phone assembly which has also been provided to the investigator. Typically, a witness will not object to this type of statement taking, but if so, acknowledge the witness' concerns and take careful notes of the interview for a written report to follow.

2.) Recording: Once the witness has given permission to record the interview, begin recording the interview and make sure to set up a separate folder with the Olympus recorder in order to maintain the integrity of the recording. Folder B or folder C should be utilized, and the entire recording should be placed into an electronic folder and e-mailed to the transcriber and to the office in order to transfer the recording to a CD Rom and be placed in the file.

Once the recorder has been turned on, repeat the identification process, stating as follows:

"This is private investigator John Jones. Today's date is September 6, 2005, and I am on the telephone with witness, Mary Smith. Mrs. Smith, would you be kind enough to state your name and spell your last name." Once the witness has done so, the following declaration should be obtained: "Mrs. Smith I have informed you that I am a private investigator, is that correct?" (Wait for affirmative response.) "And that I have also asked you for permission to record this conversation, is that correct?" (Wait for affirmative response.) "And I have your permission to do so, is that correct?" (Wait for affirmative response.)

Once the declarations and the identification are completed, ask the witness to describe what happened in a narrative, using his or her own words. During the introduction, make sure you have gone over the basic outline of the collision itself, since it is imperative that the witness is clear about the details of the collision or incident you are calling about. The witness should be allowed to use his own words to describe what he saw. It is not appropriate at this time to lead the witness, simply have him outline, in the best way he can, what he saw.

Once he has completed his narrative, it is then appropriate to ask the witness additional questions, to flesh out the basic narrative he or she has provided. Specifically, make sure that the basic, "who, what, where, when, how" are all answered. For instance, who was with the witness at the time of the collision or incident? Where was he or she standing or driving? Was the witness aware of any hazards or circumstances at the location that might have contributed to the collision or incident?

**See Appendix A – "STATEMENT GUIDE VEHICLE CRASH" – for formatted witness statement.

The investigator should have carefully reviewed the crash report or incident report prior to the phone conversation. He should be familiar with the basic location of the scene and direction and description of vehicles or location of parties prior to contacting the witness.

3) Closing: After the witness has completed answering the additional questions asked by the investigator, and the investigator is reasonably certain that everything has been elicited from the witness that he or she may have knowledge of, always ask an additional question: "Mr. Jones, is there anything that I have not asked you that you think might be important?" This may sometimes prompt the witness to recall something that he or she wanted to bring to the investigator's attention, but might have forgotten about momentarily. If there is nothing additional to add, conclude the interview by repeating the declaration from the beginning regarding permission to record the conversation. The declaration should be as follows: "Mrs. Jones, thank you for your time. Again, you are aware that I am a private investigator and that I have been recording this conversation, is that correct?" (Wait for affirmative response.) "And I have had your permission to record this conversation, is that correct?" (Wait for affirmative response.) "That will conclude my interview with Margaret Jones, witness to the collision from September 2004. Today's date is September 6, 2005, and it is 5:00 p.m." Stop the recording at this time.

Thank the witness for his or her time, and ask if it is all right if the witness can be contacted again should additional questions arise. It is important to leave the door open for witnesses to be re-contacted if new information is subsequently developed, or if the attorney has additional questions that they need clarification on.

Do not include the witness' home address or contact numbers in the recorded statement. Instead, the witness' home address, work information, and contact phone numbers should be placed in a narrative report to the attorney, reflecting the date of the interview, the fact that a recorded statement was obtained, and providing the witness' contact information. Since recorded statements are subject to discovery, it is not necessarily beneficial to the attorney to provide contact information for the witness inside the transcript of the recorded statement. Instead, that information should be maintained in a narrative report to the attorney under the work product doctrine. This permits the attorney to disclose that information about the witness when he chooses to do so, without having to turn it over with the recorded statement.

Transcripts will be released to the attorney only after being proofed by the investigator taking the statement and the supervising investigator.

CRASH INVESTIGATIONS (SCENE AND VEHICLE)

Overview

The purpose of this procedure is to provide a tickler/check list which the investigator can reference in order to observe, document and gather important investigative evidence regarding a traffic crash and pertinent facts that will provide the attorney-client with facts with which to work and upon which the trier of fact can make a decision.

This will provide investigative guidance based upon common sense and professional experience in order to provide a standardized product to our clients.

This procedure will cause the investigator to consider the instant matter/situation in light of the several procedural items offered and yield a comprehensive report.

This procedure is based upon the experiences of real life investigation. It is neither intended as the only way to conduct an investigation nor offered as a list of everything that could be done to complete the investigation of a traffic crash. This procedure offers a quick and simple method to be utilized to gather basic information. We recommend you take the time to read Frank Ritter's personal injury investigation book, *Successful Personal Injury Investigations*,

Introduction

Clients of XYZ Investigation, Inc. ("XYZ") often request XYZ to conduct an investigation into a traffic crash. XYZ's client in turn usually has their own client who has some particular interest in the traffic crash. Criminal charges might also arise from of the crash. It is helpful to know the interest of the underlying client. Although this knowledge will not change any facts, the knowledge could cause the investigator to consider the crash from a different perspective.

Generally the investigator's report will be considered attorney work product and thus potentially protected from discovery. However, it is not uncommon for the adversary to obtain a copy of the investigator's report and findings. Accordingly, the investigator should include in his/her report only factual information—not opinion or conjecture.

The investigator should expect to work in a south Florida outdoor environment. Be prepared for heat, sweat, rain and dust.

Time is of the essence when documenting facts in a traffic crash. Crash vehicles are eventually transported, sold, repaired, crushed etc. The longer the time from the crash to investigative documentation, the more likely the vehicle(s) is/are to change. The same applies to the crash scene. With time, skid marks, gouges and debris field disappear or fade. Construction work enters or leaves the scene and even traffic control devices could change over time.

Things happen for a reason. Because we live in a society governed by laws and rules, failure to follow a law or rule likely occurred in the crash being investigated. Additionally, things are designed to perform a certain function. Sometimes there are failures. Those failure(s) and its cause are to be sought by the investigator. It becomes the basis for fault, negligence and causation in the legal arena. State any such findings as possibilities in the report.

Consider the crash from a product liability perspective as well as a negligence perspective. Did a component of a vehicle fail and cause the crash or injury? Did a product within the crash scene environment, such as a traffic signal or railroad guard gate, fail and cause/contribute to the crash?

Look for any previous/recent repairs on the vehicle which could affect the performance of the vehicle or the vehicle's systems (air bag sensors not repaired properly).

Client's Theory/Needs
If possible, learn the client's theory of their case. This will assure the investigator documents facts that support or detract from that theory.

Crash Scene Documentation
When documenting a crime scene the following equipment is needed:
1. High quality single lens reflex camera and/or video
2. Flash equipment as needed
3. Measurement wheel
4. Collapsible carpenter's rule
5. Note paper
6. Diagram or aerial photograph of crash site
7. Dictation equipment
8. Safety vest
9. Flashlight

Safety of the investigator is important. At times you will be like a kid playing in traffic. Be careful and utilize safety equipment. The following points are what you need to be sure you create a crash scene report that is accurate.
- Remember: Who—What—Where—When—Why—How
- Be thoughtful and thorough, not thoughtless and rushed.
- Consider the time of day of the crash and time of day of the investigation. If possible and practical, document the crash site at the same time of day the crash occurred.
- If the investigator is photographing at night, utilize a powerful flash that is able to throw light upon distant objects of interest.
- Create a field photo log or dictation system by which the investigator can document each photograph as it is taken. This will be useful when creating a formal photograph log in the report process.
- Visualize the crash site as enclosed by a 360 degree circle.
- Minimally, the investigator needs to document the crash site from 45 degree points around that circle. Thus the investigator will capture at least eight photographs of the crash site.

- Often it will be impossible or impractical to make the circle symmetrical. However, attempt to provide the viewer with enough distance that the viewer will be able to orient the point of view with reality.
- After photographing the crash site from the eight locations, move closer to items of interest and photograph them.

Photograph the following:
1. Prominent features.
2. Street signs.
3. Route of approach to crash site. Document any warning, informational, or regulatory sign/message that the driver(s) would have encountered.
4. Traffic control devices.
5. Debris field(s).
6. Gouge marks.
7. Skid marks.
8. Items of interest dependant on the facts of the case. If, for example, the case is a pedestrian v. motor vehicle matter, capture the cross walk, sidewalk, curb areas and crossing control features.
9. Police-added paint marks at scene.

Document the following:
1. The number of lanes in the vicinity of the crash.
2. The function of the lanes in the vicinity of the crash.
3. The number and nature of traffic control features (light/signs etc).
4. The presence of crash debris.
5. The presence of skid marks.
6. Presence of roadway dividers, medians or guard rails.
7. Ditches and or waterways.
8. Cable restraints.

As an investigator, you must always consider:
- **Are there** any conflicting traffic controls or confusing features of the crash site?
- From a layman's perspective, is the roadway at the crash site adequately designed, maintained, or engineered? i.e. if the speed limit is 65 MPH (95 feet per second) it will take the average driver numerous seconds to stop for a stop light. If the traffic control light change is too fast, it may be impossible for a driver to stop.
- If the crash site is an intersection, does it appear to be controlled by computerized equipment designed to give variable control to the traffic lights?
- Are there any blind spots as a driver approaches the crash site?
- If a night crash, lighting devices and, if possible, the type (mercury, high pressure sodium, incandescent).
- Any obstructions or construction.

As an investigator, measurements are important.

- At the crash site, utilize a copy of an aerial photograph or drawing of the crash site to assist in recording locations and measurements. You will use this to create a final, well organized, professional appearing, diagram.
- Establish reference points/objects that will be present two years from today. Use these objects as measurement reference points from which to triangulate and thus show the location of an object/feature of interest. Often this information will be in the police report. If it is and appears to be reliable, use it.
- Document width of the traffic lanes
- If a curb is involved, measure the height of the curb.
- Determine distance from the apparent point of impact to prominent objects (triangulate).
- Determine distance from prominent point to debris fields
- Determine distance from point of impact (if determinable) to point of the vehicle's final resting point.
- Measure distance of items of interest (skid marks, gouge marks, paint transfer) to prominent features (triangulate).

Crash Vehicle Documentation

The following equipment will be needed:

1. High quality single lens reflex camera.
2. Two steel tapes. Keson brand makes a fine tape called a Pocket Rod. Keson also markets an accessory kit for photography. Stanley 35 foot Power Lock also works well. One inch wide tape is preferred because it stays ridged. Ridged is the key.
3. Magnets and/or small clear suction cups (used to hold tape to vehicle)
4. Device to create a straight edge. Yellow 11 foot, or longer, expandable pole used to change ceiling light bulbs is ideal. Check hardware stores to obtain. Just remove the light bulb grabber. This is used to show, in photographs, the approximate original position of body panels and associated crush/deflection/deformation.
5. Camera Tripod. This is used to hold one end of the straightedge described in 4 above.
6. Duct tape. This is used to hold measuring tapes etc. in place while photographing damage.
7. Collapsible carpenter ruler.
8. Recording device.
9. Tire pressure gauge.
10. Tire tread measuring device.

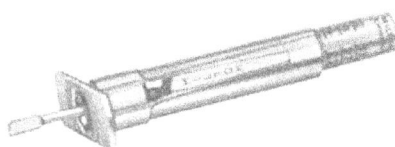

Identification of the vehicle is important:

1. Confirm VIN and/or license plate.
2. Photograph VIN. Usually the VIN tag in the driver's door area produces a better photograph than trying to shoot through the windshield at the dashboard VIN. It also identifies the manufacturing information of the vehicle if there is any product liability concern.

Other items to be considered:

- Like the crash site, envision a 360 degree circle around the vehicle and photograph it from all eight angles. Often, in a tow yard, this is very difficult. Do the best possible.
- Do not remove objects from the vehicle unless you have permission and are prepared to take the item into custody as evidence.
- Often the damage to the vehicle precludes access to, or observation of, a particular area or component of the vehicle. Do the best that you can but mention in your report that you tried. That way the client knows you exercised due diligence in your efforts.
- Remember to think product liability. Did the air bags deploy? Did a tire/wheel fail? Did the brakes fail? Did the roof collapse/fail? Did a restraint fail? Photograph the items pertinent to such an inquiry.
- Is there an "Event Data Recorder" ("black box")? If so, was it downloaded and/or does the attorney want to pursue that issue? Most small GMC and Ford vehicles have these devices.
- Measure deflection of crushed/deformed areas. Consider that an expert may be able to utilize the measurements you document to establish the energy needed to create the damage present. Place the straightedge (tape or expandable pole) where you think the original body panel would have been and measure into the current position (use the second tape or carpenters ruler). That distance is the deflection. Photograph the measurement. You will have created a "T" with the straightedge and the tape measure/ruler running from the straight edge to the current position of the body panel.
- Tires: Identify the manufacturer, model and size of each tire. Tires actually have identification numbers. Tire Identification Codes are batch codes that identify which week and year the tire was produced. Some are acutal serial numbers. The U.S. Department of Transportation (DOT) National Highway Traffic Safety Administration (NHTSA) requires that Tire Identification Code be a combination of eleven or twelve letters and numbers that identify the manufacturing location, tire size, manufacturer's code, and week and year the tire was manufactured. Finding such a number on a wrecked vehicle often proves impractical simply because you may need to crawl under the vehicle to find it on the inside of the tire. But if you need it, know that it is there.
- Indicate if the tire is inflated or not. Utilize an air pressure gauge and document the air pressure for each tire in your report.
- Measure the remaining tread on each tire. Utilize a standard tread gauge. Tire Tread Gauge MILS448 manufactured by Milton works well. Measure from the top of tread to the top of the wear bar. That will tell you the useable tread remaining on the tire. The measurement is expressed in 32^{nds} of an inch.
- Take close-up photographs of any areas of interest. What these areas are will depend on the circumstances of the crash/injury; i.e., if the air bags did not deploy, document the state of the air bag

sensors in the front of the vehicle or the side of the vehicle. If a tire failed take close up photographs of the tires, etc.

- Wheel assemblies should be documented and photographed. If a wheel assembly broke or failed it could have caused a crash.
- Check the condition, position and functionality of the seats. Did the seat back fail, etc.?
- Check the condition and functionality of the seat belt and buckle/clip/release mechanism. If the belt is cut, report that.
- Document the condition of the interior passenger compartments. Any apparent impact between the occupants and roof etc.?

Police Reports

- Obtain and carefully review any police reports.
- Before going to a crash site, be sure you understand what is reported to have happened.
- It is not unusual to find errors in the report. Include a discussion of any errors in your report.
- Note if anyone was issued citations and if so—what violation is alleged.

Investigative Reports

- Write the investigative report in the first person: "I did this and that".
- Capture who did what, when, where, why and how; i.e. 'On January 3, 2007, I went to the intersection of First Street and North Pearl Street, Fort Walton Beach, Florida, 33456. At that location I searched for a crash site reportedly involving...'
- Include all observations that are pertinent to the matter.
- Include any drawings of the crash scene in the report.
- Include in the report a table of the photographs. Indicate what the photograph shows and assign each photograph a unique number for identification. The photographs should be labeled. The photograph number and label must coincide with this chart.
- Do not include any conjecture or conclusions unless you are writing the report as an expert. Likely that will not be the case, so just state the facts. Others will interpret what you observed.

REPORT PREPARATION (CIVIL AND CRIMINAL)

It is the policy of XYZ Investigations, Inc. that staff investigators dictate reports of all activities conducted during the course of assigned investigations. It is impractical and non-productive for a professional investigator to sit and type reports when resources are available to type and review a dictated report.

1. The investigator takes notes from the completed interview or task. Using the company provided digital recorder, the investigator will dictate, in a narrative style, the content of the information obtained. Review the **Format** for each particular report type, i.e. assets check, client/witness interview, field canvass.

    a. The attorney's name shall be provided, along with the case reference, i.e.: "*This report is for Mitchell Beers, Esq. The case reference is State v. Mahoney, case number 2018CF1040A. This is an interview of Warren Stafford.*" (It may be necessary to provide the attorney's address, unless the transcriber already has this information.)

    b. The narrative shall follow the report **format**, samples of which are included in this manual.

    c. The signature line shall be provided at the end of the report, e.g., "*Submitted by Mark Murnan, Licensed Private Investigator.*"

2. Reports shall be compiled in a single digital file for transfer to the transcriptionist.

3. Reports shall be forwarded, via e-mail, to the transcriptionist at the end of each business day.

4. Once the reports have been typed, the transcriptionist shall e-mail the draft reports to the investigator for review.

5. The investigator shall review and make any changes to the draft report.

6. Once the review has been completed, the report shall be e-mailed to the office manager and placed into the "drafts" computer folder for review by the office manager.

7. Once the office manager has reviewed the reports for grammar and punctuation, the case manager will next review the reports for content and form and place the completed reports into the "Proofs" computer folder for printing and mailing/emailing.

8. The administrative assistant will print the reports, make copies of the reports for the investigative file, and disburse the reports to the recipient, being sure to include all attachments.

9. The administrative assistant will file a copy of the report in the investigative file.

STATEMENT GUIDE VEHICLE CRASH - WITNESS

The following is offered as a guide to assist the investigator in the interview process. It should not be used as a "word for word" substitute for obtaining the narrative or establishing a rapport with the witness. Instead, consider it a checklist to ensure that all pertinent information has been obtained from the witness.

Opening

This is private investigator (name of investigator) conducting a recorded interview ("in person" or "by telephone") with (name of person being interviewed) on (date of interview) concerning an incident which took place on (date of incident) at (location of incident). I am working on behalf of (name of attorney), who represents (name of plaintiff).

Permission

1. Do you understand that this interview is being recorded?
2. Is it being recorded with your permission?

Identification

1. Would you state your full name, and spell your last name, please?
2. What is your date of birth?
3. What is your home address?
4. How long have you lived there? Do you have any plans to move in the near future?
5. What is your home, cell, and work telephone numbers?
6. What is your marital status?
7. What is your spouse's name?

Employment/Education

1. Where are you employed?
2. How long have you worked there?
3. What is your work number? Address?
4. What kind of work do you do?
5. What is your educational background? (High school, college, technical school)

Future Contact

1. Can I, or the attorney I work with, contact you in the future?
2. What is the best number to reach you?

Vehicle Crash Date. Location. Weather & Road Conditions

1. Did you witness a vehicle crash on (Date)?
2. Please tell me what you saw (have the witness give a narrative version of what they saw).

- What was the time of the vehicle crash?

3. Where were you positioned in the roadway when you witnessed the vehicle crash?
   - How far from the point of impact were you located?

4. What were the weather conditions?
   - Were the windshield wipers on? (Raining)
   - Were the headlights on? (Raining, dark or night)

5. Exactly where did the vehicle crash occur? (Intersection, side of road, which lane?)
6. Describe the vehicles that were involved in this crash.
   - How many vehicles were involved?
   - What make were the vehicles?
   - What color were the vehicles?

7. Describe the road and area where vehicle crash occurred.
   - How many lanes of travel on the road?
   - What is the posted speed limit on the road?
   - Was there any construction work being done to the road?
   - Any medians, trees, or landscaping that might impact visibility?

8. Were you in a vehicle yourself? Did you have a passenger? Who? (Name and telephone number, address) Where were they seated in your vehicle?

9. Where were you going? Where were you coming from?

10. How often do you travel this roadway? How familiar are you with the roadway?

11. Did you have the radio on?

12. Were your windows up or down?

13. Could you hear anything prior to the impact? (Brakes screeching, horns honking)

14. Were there any traffic controls (stop sign, traffic light, etc) where this vehicle crash took place?
    - What type of traffic controls were there?
    - What type of traffic controls did the vehicles have when this vehicle crash occurred?

15. Describe any conditions or objects which may have obstructed your view (trees, landscaping, median, construction).

16.   Describe any objects which may have obstructed any of the drivers' views (trees, landscaping, median, construction).

Speed

1.   How fast were you traveling at that time?

2.   How fast were each of the colliding vehicles traveling at the time of impact?

Vehicle Crash Details

1.   Describe to me what happened prior to and during the vehicle crash.

2.   What effort if any, was made by the drivers to avoid the vehicle crash?

3.   What was the position of the two vehicles just prior to impact?

4.   What was their respective position at the time of impact?
  • Describe the impact and points of contact.

5.   What was the position of each vehicle after the collision?

6.   Was anything else struck by either vehicle after the initial impact?

7.   Were there any visible skid marks on the street or road surface?
  • Did anyone measure them?
    • Who measured them?
    • How long were the marks?

8.   What is your relationship (if any) to the drivers involved in this vehicle crash?

Vehicle Damage

1.   Describe the damage to the vehicles.
  • Where was the damage located on the vehicles?
  • Were either/any of the cars driveable after the vehicle crash?

2.   Were the cars towed from the vehicle crash scene?
  • What wrecker company moved them?

Seat Belts

1.   Were the vehicles equipped with seat belts?
  • Were either of the drivers wearing their seat belts?

Fault for the Crash

1. Do you agree that this crash was 100% the fault of the driver (name the defendant and identify the car the defendant was driving)? Why? Or why not?

2. Do you agree that name of plaintiff was not at fault? (Identify the vehicle plaintiff was driving) Why? Or why not?

3. Do you believe any other person or factor was responsible for causing the crash (i.e., road construction, road design, defective vehicles, debris, another driver, etc.)?

4. Did anyone receive a ticket/traffic citation for this crash, that you know of?
    *   What was the ticket for (careless driving, speeding, failure to yield)?

5. Did you attend a court hearing as a result of this crash? Did you receive a subpoena to appear as a witness? Do you have a copy of the subpoena?

6. Was there any indication that either of the drivers had been drinking? (if so, who, and what indications?)

Alcohol and Eyewear

1. Had you been drinking any alcoholic beverages or taking any prescription medication prior to seeing the vehicle crash? IF YES,
    *   Where did you drink the alcohol?
    *   How much alcohol did you consume?
    *   What medication did you take?
    *   How long prior to seeing the vehicle crash?

2. Do you have any condition which might affect your ability to see or recall the events you're telling me about?

3. Do you wear corrective lenses or eye glasses?
    *   Were you wearing them when you saw the vehicle crash?

Passengers

1. Did either driver have any passengers in their vehicle?
    *   What are their names, ages, addresses and telephone numbers?
    *   Where were they seated in the vehicle?

Witnesses

1. Were there any other witnesses to this vehicle crash?
    *   What are their names, ages, addresses and telephone numbers?
2. Where were they located when they saw the vehicle crash?

Police Investigation / Post Vehicle crash Discussions

1. Were the police contacted after the incident?
   - Who contacted the police?
2. Who investigated the incident? (City police, sheriff, or state patrol)
3. Did either driver receive a citation?
4. What was the outcome?
5. Did you overhear any conversation between the police officer and the drivers?
   - What was said in each conversation?
6. Did you have any conversation with the drivers, passengers or other witnesses?
   - What was said in each conversation?

Injuries

1. Was anyone injured in this vehicle crash?
   - Who was injured?
   - What type of injuries did they have?
   - Were they transported to a hospital?
   - Who transported them?

Closing:

1. Is there anything you would like to add regarding this incident?
2. Have you understood all of the questions asked?
3. Is all of the information that you have given true and correct?
4. Do you understand that this interview has been recorded?
5. Was it recorded with your permission?
6. May I contact you again if we need any additional information?
7. Thank you. The time is now _____. This concludes our interview.

STATEMENT GUIDE: SLIP AND FALL - WITNESS

Opening

This is private investigator (name of investigator) conducting a recorded interview ("in person" or "by telephone") with (name of person being interviewed) on (date of interview) concerning an incident which took place on (date of incident) at (location of incident). I am working on behalf of (name of attorney), who represents (name of plaintiff).

Permission

1.   Do you understand that this interview is being recorded?
2.   Is it being recorded with your permission?

Identification

1.   Would you state your full name, and spell your last name, please?
2.   What is your date of birth?
3.   What is your home address?
4.   How long have you lived there? Do you have any plans to move in the near future?
5.   What is your home, cell, and work telephone numbers?
6.   What is your marital status?
   • What is your spouse's name?

Employment/Education

1.   Where are you employed?
2.   How long have you worked there?
3.   What is your work number? Address?
4.   What kind of work do you do?
5.   What is your educational background? (High school, college, technical school)

Future Contact

1.   Can I, or the attorney I work with, contact you in the future?
2.   What is the best number to reach you?

Narrative

1.   Describe in a narrative fashion what happened, how the client slipped/tripped/fell.

2.   Identify the client:
   a.   How known (relationship, if any)
   b.   Describe the client
      1.   Male/female, height, weight

    2.   Clothing

    3.   Shoes (heels, flip-flops, running shoes)

    4.   Describe soles, if known (rubber, leather)

3.   Why was client at the scene/location?

    a.   Guest/licensee (social guest at a home or business) of owner?

    b.   Invitee or business visitor (shopping or doing business at location)?

    c.   Trespasser (no actual or implied consent by owner)?

4.   Location of the slip/trip/fall incident:

    a.   Common stairway or private stairway (secured/locked)?

    b.   Sidewalk? Public or private?

    c.   Apartment or commercial building?

    d.   Exact location where client fell (parking space, pothole, step, curb, etc.)

5.   How often did the client frequent the location?

    a.   Daily? only on this occasion?

6.   Defects:

    a.   What caused the slip/trip/fall?

    b.   Describe the cause (water, oil, loose rock/gravel, debris, parking stop, etc.)

    c.   Describe the location of the defect (aisle of a store, parking space, curb, outside/inside step)

    d.   If a step or stairwell:

        1.   Any defect to the step (broken, crumbling, cracks)?

        2.   Any cohesive strips or grading to enhance traction?

    e.   Did the defect cause the fall?

7.   Notice:

    a.   Did the property owner know of the defect? Should he/she have known of the defect? (Ongoing rain in area, location in obvious disrepair, leaking refrigeration/air conditioning unit, broken bottles, leaves and debris falling from trees, etc.)

    b.   Did property owner take any action to provide warning about the defect? (i.e., yellow cones, warning barricades, closing off area)

    c.   If so, what?

    d.   If no action taken, what should have been done?

8.   Lighting:

    a.   What type of lighting in vicinity of defect? (Natural/sunlight, fluorescent, light bulbs)

    b.   Was lighting sufficient for the environment? (i.e. dim bulb over doorway, no lights in parking lot, broken or inoperative light fixtures)

    c.   Did lighting illuminate defect?

    d.   Did lack of light contribute to fall? How so?

9.   Describe how client fell

    a.   Foot/Feet slip out from under

    b.   Fall forward? Backward? To the side?

    c.   Twisted ankle/knee?

    d.   How did client land?

         1.   On back or backside, on side, strike back of head, face first?

10.   Describe injuries sustained

    a.   Injuries to knee, ankle, back, head?

    b.   Broken bones, lacerations to face/head/limbs?

11.   Prior injuries

    a.   Had client ever injured this part of his/her body before?

    b.   Previous or pre-existing condition which might have contributed to this fall?

12.   Other issues

    a.   In case of stairwell, was there a bannister or hand rail?

         1.   Was it intact, stable or loose?

    b.   Was the client in a hurry? Where was he/she going?

    c.   Was client carrying something in his/her arms or hands? If so, what and why?

13.   Identify other witnesses

    a.   Who else was present or responded to the scene?

    b.   Did anyone make any comments about the defect or the fall itself?

         1.   If so, what was said?

14.   Post-fall

    a.   Who contacted management/owner?

    b.   What did manager/owner say?

    c.   Did management/security/owner take an incident report?

    d.   Was there a video surveillance system present at the location (department stores or convenience stores, parking lots, common areas)?

    e.   What did management/security/owner do after being notified of the fall?

         1.   Call for maintenance to clean or correct defect?

         2.   Place cones or warning signs at location?

         3.   Ignore defect or blame client?

Closing

1.   Is there anything you would like to add regarding this incident?
2.   Have you understood all of the questions I've asked you?
3.   Is all of the information you've given me true and correct?
4.   Do you understand that this interview has been recorded?
5.   Has it been recorded with your permission?

Thank you, this concludes our interview. Today's date is _____ and the time is _____.

ABOUT THE AUTHORS

Mark J. Murnan (President, Chief Investigator) is a Certified Legal Investigator (CLI®) and a Certified Fraud Examiner (CFE®). Mark served in the United States Air Force, where he attended the Defense Language Institute at the Presidio of Monterey. He received his Bachelor degree in criminal justice at the University of Nebraska at Omaha. Mark is a former staff investigator for the Federal Public Defender, Southern District of Florida. He has over 35 years of investigative experience in both the public and private sectors. He has assisted counsel in cases of securities and wire fraud, money laundering, drug trafficking, murder, sexual battery, and gang-related crimes. As one of only a few Certified Legal Investigators in the country, Mark has also assisted civil counsel in the litigation of negligence cases, wrongful death claims, premises and products liability cases, and estate and probate matters. He has written extensively for professional journals and lectured on investigative procedures in the classroom and at conferences. He is the past president of the Florida Association of Licensed Investigators (FALI), one of the largest private investigator associations in the country. He is the former Regional Director for the southeast United States for the National Association of Legal Investigators (NALI).

Wendy E. Murnan, LPI, CP, FRP – Vice-President; Licensed Private Investigator; Certified Paralegal. Wendy is a private investigator and nationally certified paralegal. She is also a registered paralegal with The Florida Bar. Wendy has over 40 years of experience in the legal arena. Before entering the private field, Wendy worked 16 years for nationally renowned attorney, Robert M. Montgomery, Jr., in West Palm Beach, Florida, as his private paralegal and assistant. She assisted with many landmark cases while working with Montgomery, including *Kimberly Bergalis vs. David Acer, DDS*; a case in which a dentist infected five of his patients with the AIDS virus; and *State of Florida vs. American Tobacco Co.*, a case which resulted in a billion dollar settlement for the plaintiff. Wendy became an expert in handling and organizing large document cases. Her knowledge of civil procedures and the issues involved in complex litigation make her a valuable asset to our attorneys preparing for trial. As an investigator, Wendy specializes in research, including complex background and asset investigations. Her "scorched earth" due diligence has uncovered invaluable information for our attorney clients over the years. Wendy also specializes in obtaining crucial records and documents needed by the attorneys in order that they have the complete information they need to effectually represent their clients.

www.ingramcontent.com/pod-product-compliance
Lightning Source LLC
Chambersburg PA
CBHW080602030426
42336CB00019B/3304